George Washington's Secret Ally

By Hon. Edward F. Butler, Sr.
with David W. Swafford, editor

Copyright © 2016 Southwest Historic Press
All rights reserved. 1st paperback printing 2016

Library of Congress Cataloging-in-Publication Data
Butler, Judge Ed

Judge Ed Butler - 1st ed.

George Washington's Secret Ally

Edward F. Butler, Sr., with David W. Swafford
107 pages

ISBN NO: 978-1-532-31601-2

Published by
Southwest Historic Press
San Antonio, TX
Tel.

1. United States - History - Revolution, 1775-1783 - Participation, Spanish. 2. United States - Foreign relations - 1774-1783. 3. United States - Foreign relations - Spain. 4. Spain - Foreign relations - Spain. 4. Spain - Foreign relations - United States.

Dedication

To HRM Felipe VI de Borbón, King of Spain, who requested I spread the word about Spain's valuable assistance to the Patriot cause in the American Revolution.

-Ed Butler

Editor's Note

Parts of the ensuing text on Spain's contribution to the American Revolution (pp. 44 – 90) were originally published in consecutive issues of the SONS Drumbeat, the quarterly membership newsletter of the **General Society, Sons of the Revolution.**

The GSSR has granted the Southwest Historic Press permission for reproducing the work as one volume.

The facts and storyline presented herein are based on the author's book, *"Gálvez/Spain, Our Forgotten Ally in the American Revolutionary War: A Concise Summary of Spain's Assistance."* To order a copy of that book, please see order form on p. 93.

About the Author

Judge Ed Butler

Judge Edward F. Butler, Sr. is a retired U.S. Administrative Law Judge. Before serving in that position he served as Presiding Municipal Judge for South Padre Island, Texas. He is an honor graduate of Vanderbilt University School of Law, which he attended as a Ford Foundation Scholar. He was a board certified civil trial lawyer before assuming full time duties on the bench. He is the author of thirteen books, three of which are on family history.

Judge Butler is a frequent seminar and after dinner speaker on historical and genealogical topics, and is a regular contributor to national and state historical and genealogical society journals and magazines. Since his retirement in 1997, he has devoted considerable time and energy to the National Society Sons of the American Revolution, where he served as President General, and Chairman of the Board of the SAR Foundation.

In March 2001, then SAR President General Larry D. McClanahan, appointed Judge Butler as the SAR Ambassador to México and Latin America. Judge Butler's interest in Spain's assistance to the colonists in the American Revolutionary War stems from his participation with the SAR in México for which he was the founder and Charter President. In 2010 he also founded the SAR Society in Spain.

Judge Butler previously served as Genealogist General of the national SAR before which he served as Genealogist for the Texas Society, SAR. He served for seven years as a member of the National SAR genealogy committee. He served for two years as genealogical editor of *The Texas Compatriot*, magazine of the Texas Society of SAR. He also published a monthly column for SAR chapter newsletters, entitled "The Genealogy Corner." He was the author of the monthly historical column, "Remembering Yesterday," carried in many Texas newspapers.

Judge Ed Butler was the 2009-2010 President General, National Society Sons of the American Revolution. In July 2011 he was made an Honorary Member of the Order of the Granaderos y Damas de Gálvez. In July 2012 he was the founder and Charter Grand Viscount General of the Order of the Founders of North America 1492-1692, and served as its charter Grand Viscount General. His accomplishments have earned him inclusion in *Who's Who in the World* (Marquis 2011), *Who's Who in America* (2010), *Who's Who in American Law, Who's Who in the South and Southwest, Who's Who in Practicing Attorneys* (1989), *Who's Who in*

Texas, Dictionary of International Biographies, and *2000 Notable Americans.* He has been honored as an Admiral in the Texas Navy, Tennessee Colonel, Kentucky Colonel, and as an Arkansas Traveler. He has been the recipient of Keys to the Cities of Memphis, TN and Birmingham, AL.

Other groups in which Judge Ed Butler has actively participated include:

- México Society, Sons of the American Revolution (Founder, Charter President)
- Spain Society, Sons of the American Revolution (Founder, Charter Chancellor)
- France Society, Sons of the American Revolution - Honorary President General (2010)
- Children of the American Revolution - Honorary Vice President General (2009-2010)
- SAR Conference on the American Revolution - Founding Board Member
- Military Order of the Knights of the Temple of Jerusalem (Deputy Grand Prior; Grand Croix)
- Raymond J. Davis Foundation of the Knights Templar - Board Member 2003-present

- General Society of the Colonial Wars (Deputy Governor General 2012-2014)
- Society of the Descendants of Washington's Army at Valley Forge (Judge Advocate General)
- Order of the First Families of Maryland, President, Texas Society (2013-2014); Chancellor General (2014- present)
- George Washington Foundation - Fellow (2001-present)
- General Society of the War of 1812 (Judge Advocate General)
- Military Order of the Stars and Bars (Deputy Judge Advocate General)
- General Society Sons of Revolution (President of the Texas Society; Vice President General)
- Order of the Founder and Patriots of America (Governor of the Texas Society)
- Magna Charta Dames and Barons (Vice Regent of the Texas Society; Regent of the San Antonio Colony)
- Reserve Officers Association (Navy Vice President Tennessee and Texas)
- Navy Reserve Association (President of Mississippi Valley Chapter)
- Military Order of Foreign Wars (President of Memphis, TN Chapter)

- Sons of Confederate Veterans (Texas Division Parliamentarian; Camp Commander)
- Texas Chapter, Royal Society of St. George (Founding Secretary)
- Judge Butler is also a member of the following groups:
- Sons of the Republic of Texas (Honorary Member, Tyler, TX Chapter)
- Order of the *Granaderos y Damas de Gálvez* (Honorary Member)
- *Los Bexarenos* Genealogical and Historical Society.
- Sovereign Colonial Society Americans of Royal Descent
- Colonial Order of the Crown
- Plantagenet Society
- Order of Americans of Armorial Ancestry
- Military Order of the World Wars
- Society of Descendants of Knights of the Most Noble Order of the Garter
- Military Order of the Crusades
- Order of the Crown of Charlemagne in the United States of America
- National Huguenot Society
- Sons and Daughters of the Colonial and Antebellum Bench and Bar
- Gavel Club
- Boonesboro Society
- Alamo Defenders Descendants Soc.

- Order of the First Families of North Carolina
- Travelers Century Club (Silver level member, for those who have traveled to 150 countries or more). The author has visited 180 countries accepted by TCC.
- The Circumnavigators Society

About the Editor

David W. Swafford

Mr. Swafford has worked as a writer-editor for over thirty years and holds a degree in journalism from the University of Kansas. Since 2008, he has edited the international quarterly newsletter of the General Society, Sons of the Revolution—a major lineage society of descendants of Revolutionary War patriots. Additionally, he has co-authored or ghostwritten a growing number of memoirs, business books and other manuscripts.

David is an experienced newspaper reporter and copy editor, magazine editor and writer, marketing and communications specialist, broadcast script writer, and ESL/EFL language instructor.

In addition to his role as contractual editor for the GSSR, he is currently serving as Vice President & Secretary of the Missouri Society, Sons of the Revolution.

He is well traveled in the United States, Mexico and Latin America and speaks fluent Spanish. Mr. Swafford has received accolades for his skills from teachers, employers, and clients. His personal interests include history, genealogy, creative writing, and martial arts. He resides in Kansas City, Missouri and may be reached at **dwsnarratives@gmail.com**

Table of Contents

Title Page 3
Copyright Page 4
Dedication 5
Editor's Note 6
About the Author 7
About the Editor 14
Table of Contents 16
Table of Illustrations 18
Foreword 20
George Washington's Secret Ally 22
Two Telling Letters 27
The Gathering Storm 34
The Winds of War 38
Old World Background 44
Early Spanish Involvement 50
France Declares War on Britain 57

Table of Contents (cont'd)

A European Front 59

The Western Theater 62

Clark's Spanish Friends 67

Britain's Grand Design 70

Gen. Bernardo de Gálvez—Hero 75

The Texas Connection to the Revolution 82

Spain Declares War 84

Next Target: West Florida 87

In Retrospect 90

Want to Know More? 92

Order Form 94

Endnotes 95

List of Illustrations

Judge Edward F. Butler, Sr., Author 7

David W. Swafford, Editor 14

Judge Ed Butler, wife Robin, & King Felipe ... 21

English Pirates Attacking Spanish Ships 37

Charles III of Spain 44

Ferdinand VI of Spain 45

Louis XV of France 47

1779 Engraving, "The Family Compact" 48

Maps showing Louisiana territory transferred from France to Spain in 1763 49

Benjamin Franklin 51

Pierre Augustin Caron de Beaumarchais 53

Diego Gardoqui 53

Coat of Arms of Spanish Louisiana 56

Louis XVI of France 58

John Paul Jones 59

1704 Engraving, View of Gibraltar 61

List of Illustrations
(cont'd)

Don Bernardo de Gálvez 63

Depiction, Early Saint Louis 66

Francis Vigo, USPS Commemorative 69

1790s Map, Early Saint Louis 72

Battle of San Carlos Mural 74

Rendering, San Juan Nepomuceno 77

Old Havana and Cathedral 79

First Church of Saint Louis, New Orleans 83

Gen. John Campbell, of Starchur 84

Capt. Elias Walker Durnford 86

1767 Map of West Florida 88

Battle of Pensacola 89

Gálvez Pedestal (Yo Solo) 91

Ed Butler Book Cover 92

Forward

In May 2010, HRM Felipe VI de Borbón, the current King of Spain, asked me to write a book about Spain's vital assistance during the American Revolutionary War. In 2015, I published the award winning book, *Gálvez / Spain - Our Forgotten Ally in the American Revolutionary War: A Concise Summary of Spain's Assistance.*

Subsequently, The General Society Sons of the Revolution (GSSR) published a three-part series of articles on the themes presented in my book. The articles ran in successive issues of the Sons' quarterly magazine, The SONS *Drumbeat*, (2015-2016), and are presented here in a contiguous format. The publication is edited by David W. Swafford.

On a recent book tour through the southeast U.S., I had several people asking me for a shorter version of my book. This book responds to that request.

Robin Butler and Judge Ed Butler chat with King Felipe following the formal royal audience.

Spain: George Washington's Secret Ally

THE BEST PROOF OF THIS LITTLE-KNOWN TRUTH WAS WHEN THE U.S. CONGRESS MADE BERNARDO DE GÁLVEZ, SPANISH VISCOUNT TO NEW SPAIN, AN HONORARY CITIZEN OF THE UNITED STATES:

ONE HUNDRED THIRTEENTH CONGRESS OF THE UNITED STATES OF AMERICA

AT THE SECOND SESSION

Begun and held at the City of Washington on Friday, the third day of January, two thousand and fourteen

H. J. RES. 105

JOINT RESOLUTION

Conferring honorary citizenship of the United States on Bernardo de Gálvez y Madrid, Viscount of Galveston and Count of Gálvez.

Whereas the United States has conferred honorary citizenship on 7 other occasions during its history, and honorary citizenship is and should remain an extraordinary honor not lightly conferred nor frequently granted;

Whereas Bernardo de Gálvez y Madrid, Viscount of Galveston and Count of Gálvez, was a hero of the Revolutionary War who risked his life for the freedom of the United States people and provided supplies, intelligence, and strong military support to the war effort;

Whereas Bernardo de Gálvez recruited an army of 7,500 men made up of Spanish, French, African-American, Mexican, Cuban, and Anglo-American forces and led the effort of Spain to aid the United States' colonists against Great Britain;

Whereas during the Revolutionary War, Bernardo de Gálvez and his troops seized the Port of New Orleans and successfully defeated the British at battles in Baton Rouge, Louisiana, Natchez, Mississippi, and Mobile, Alabama;

Whereas Bernardo de Gálvez led the successful 2-month Siege of Pensacola, Florida, where his troops captured the capital of British West Florida and left the British with no naval bases in the Gulf of Mexico;

Whereas Bernardo de Gálvez was wounded during the Siege of Pensacola, demonstrating bravery that forever endeared him to the United States soldiers;

Whereas Bernardo de Gálvez' victories against the British were recognized by George Washington as a deciding factor in the outcome of the Revolutionary War;

Whereas Bernardo de Gálvez helped draft the terms of treaty that ended the Revolutionary War;

Whereas the United States Continental Congress declared, on October 31, 1778, their gratitude and favorable sentiments to Bernardo de Gálvez for his conduct towards the United States;

Whereas after the war, Bernardo de Gálvez served as viceroy of New Spain and led the effort to chart the Gulf of Mexico, including Galveston Bay, the largest bay on the Texas coast;

Whereas several geographic locations, including Galveston Bay, Galveston, Texas, Galveston County, Texas, Gálvez, Louisiana, and St. Bernard Parish, Louisiana, are named after Bernardo de Gálvez;

Whereas the State of Florida has honored Bernardo de Gálvez with the designation of Great Floridian; and

Whereas Bernardo de Gálvez played an integral role in the Revolutionary War and helped secure the independence of the United States: Now, therefore, be it

That Bernardo de Gálvez y Madrid, Viscount of Galveston and Count of Gálvez, is proclaimed posthumously to be an honorary citizen of the United States.

Speaker of the House of Representatives.

Vice President of the United States and President of the Senate.

Two Telling Letters:

1) T. Jefferson to B. Gálvez

Williamsburg November 8th. 1779

SIR,
By Mr. Lindsay who was sent from our County of Illinois on the Mississippi to new Orleans and lately arrived here on his return by the way of Havana, we hear that Col. Rogers had left New Orleans and proceeded up the Mississippi; We are anxiously expecting by him your Excellency's answer to the Letters of January 14 1778 by Col. Rogers and January 26th. 1778 by Captain Young from Governor Henry to whom I had the honor of succeeding on his Resignation.

The Accession of his most Catholic Majesty, since the Date of those Letters to the Hostilities carrying on by the confederate powers of France and North America against Great Britain, thereby adding to their efforts, the weight of your powerful and wealthy Empire, has given us, all the certainty of a happy Issue to the present Contest, of which human Events will admit.

Our Vicinity to the State over which you immediately preside; the direct channel of Commerce by the River Mississippi, the nature of those Commodities with which we can reciprocally furnish each other, point out the advantages which may result from a close Connection, and correspondence, for which on our part the best Foundations are laid by a grateful Sense of the Favors we have received at your Hands.

Notwithstanding the pressure of the present War on our people, they are lately beginning to extend their Settlements rapidly on the Waters of the Mississippi; and we have reason to believe, that on the Ohio particularly, and the Branches immediately communicating with it, there will in the Course of another Year, be such a number of Settlers, as to render the Commerce an object worth your notice.

From New Orleans alone can they be tolerably suppl[ied] with necessaries of European Manufactures, and thither they will carry in Exchange Staves and Peltry immediately, and Flour pork and Beef, as soon as they shall have somewhat opened their Lands.

For their Protection from the Indians, we are obliged to send and station among them, a considerable armed Force; the providing of which with cloathing, and the Friendly Indians with necessaries, becomes a matter of great Difficulty with us.

For the smaller Forces we have hitherto kept up at Kaskaskia on the Mississippi we have contracted a considerable Debt at New Orleans with Mr. Pollock, besides what is due to your State for the Supplies they have generously furnished, and a Number of Bills from Col. Clarke now lying under protest in New Orleans.

We learn by Mr. Lindsay that Mr. Pollock is likely to be greatly distress'd, if we do not immediately make him remittances. The most unfavorable Harvest ever known Since the Settlement of this Country, has put it out of our Power to send flour, obliging us for our own subsistence, to purchase it from the neighboring States of Maryland and Pennsylvania to whom we have until this Year furnished large Quantities.

The Want of Salt disables us from preparing Beef and Pork for your market. In this Situation of things, we cannot but contemplate the distress of that Gentleman brought on him by Services rendered us, with the utmost Concern.

We are endeavoring by Remittances of Tobacco to establish a Fund in France to which we may apply to a certain extent: But the Casualties to which those Tobaccos are liable in their Transportation; render the Dependence less certain than we could wish for Mr. Pollock's relief; and besides that we have other very extensive occasions for them.

Young as we are in Trade and Manufactures, and engaged in war with a Nation whose power on the Sea, has been such as to intercept a great proportion of the Supplies we have attempted to import from Europe, you will not wonder to hear, that we find great Difficulties in procuring either money or Commodities to answer the Calls of our Armies, and therefore that it would be a Circumstance of vast relief to us, if we could leave our deposits in France for the Calls of that part of our State which lies on the Atlantic, and procure a Suspension of the Demands from Your Quarter, for supplies to our Western Forces one, Two, or three Years, or such longer Time as could be obtained; With this view Governor Henry in his Letters of January 14 and 26th 1778 solicited from Your Nation a loan of money which your Excellency was so kind, as to undertake to communicate to Your Court.

The Success of this application we expect to learn by Col. Rogers, and should not till then have troubled you with the same Subject, had we not heard of Mr. Pollock's distress. As we flatter ourselves that the Application thro' the intervention of your Excellency may have been successful, and that you may be authorized to advance for us some loans in money, I take the Liberty of soliciting you in such Case, to advance for us to Mr. Pollock Sixty five Thousand Eight Hundred fourteen & ⅝ Dollars.

Encompassed as we are with Difficulties, we may fail in doing as much as our Gratitude would prompt us to, in speedily replacing these Aids; But most assuredly nothing in that way within our Power will be left undone. Our particular prospects for doing it, and the time it may take to accomplish the whole, shall be the Subject of another Letter, as soon as I shall have the Honor to learn from you whether we can be supplied, and to what extent.

By Col. Rogers I hope also to learn your Excellency's Sentiments, on the Other proposition in the Same Letters, for the establishment of corresponding Posts on Your Side and ours of the Mississippi, near the mouth of the Ohio, for the promotion of Commerce

Between us. After returning our most cordial thanks to your Excellency for the friendly Disposition you have personally shewn to us, and, assuring you of our profound Respect and Esteem, beg Leave to Subscribe myself, Your Excellency's most obedient, and most humble Servant,

      Th: Jefferson

2) G. Washington to G. Morris

Fish-Kill, 4 October 1779

Dear Sir,

Excerpt: "If the Spaniards would but join their Fleets to those of France, & commence hostilities, my doubts would all subside—without it, I fear the British Navy has it too much in its power to counteract the schemes of France…

"If you have any news worth communicating, do not put it under a bushel, but give it to, dear Sir, yours sincerely, &c."

George Washington

The Gathering Storm[1]

For hundreds of years before the American Revolutionary War, there was bad blood between England and Spain. The two countries were at war with each other more often than not. The following chronological list of wars and battles illustrates the point:

1337-1453	The Hundred Years' War. Aragon, Castile and Majorca were allied with France against England.
1381-1382	3rd Ferdinand War. England was allied with Portugal against Castile.
1383-1385	Crises between England and Castile
1508-1516	War of the League of Cambria, a conflict in Italy, a.k.a. the War of the Holy League.
1526-1530	War of the League of Cognac, between England and Spain.
1568-1648	Eighty Years' War
1579-1583	Second Desmond Rebellion

1585-1604	First Anglo Spanish War
1588	The sinking of the Spanish Armada by the English
1589	The destruction of the remainder of the Spanish fleet and the capture of Cádiz by England.
1594-1603	Nine Years' War
1602-1663	Dutch-Portuguese War
1618-1648	Thirty Years' War
1625-1630	Second Anglo-Spanish War
1635-1659	Franco-Spanish War
1640-1668	Portuguese Restoration War
1654-1660	Third Anglo-Spanish War. This war started by Oliver Cromwell's attack on Spanish holdings in the Caribbean, Europe, and the Canary Islands. That war was concluded by the 1670 Treaty of Madrid in which Spain lost Jamaica to England.
1672-1678	Franco-Dutch War

1701-1714	War of Spanish Succession. Spain was divested of its possessions in Europe outside the Iberian Peninsula.
1702-1713	Queen Anne's War
1718-1720	War of Quadruple Alliance
1727-1729	Third Anglo-Spanish War
1739-1748	War of Jenkins' Ear
1740-1748	War of Austrian Succession
1756-1763	Seven Years' War, a.k.a. French & Indian War
1761	The "Borbón Family Compact" between Carlos III of Spain and his young nephew, Louis XVI of France, provided that if any nation attacked either France or Spain, the other could be called upon to render military or naval aid.
1762-1763	Fourth Anglo-Spanish War, a part of the Seven Years' War.

From the above we can see that during the 439 years between 1337 and 1776, Spain and England were at war for 264 years and at peace for only 175 years. In addition to the wars, English pirates and privateers continuously captured Spanish merchant ships laden with silver and gold from the Americas and precious goods from the Philippines and Asia. Clearly, there was bad blood between the two nations.

English pirates continuously attacked Spanish ships

The Winds of War[2]

The American Revolutionary War did not begin overnight. The first seeds of conflict were sewn with the signing of the 1763 Treaty of Paris, which concluded the Seven Years' War, a.k.a., the French and Indian War.[3]

The Treaty of Paris ultimately set the Thirteen Colonies on the path toward seeking their independence from Great Britain. That path culminated with the signing of the Declaration of Independence in 1776.

During the Seven Years' War, Britain captured the French Caribbean islands of Martinique, Guadeloupe, and St. Lucia. Britain also captured Havana, Cuba and Manila, Philippines from Spain.

The Treaty of Paris redistributed lands in North America accordingly:

- French lands west of the Mississippi River went to Spain, and those east of the Mississippi went to Great Britain.

- Spain retained Cuba and The Philippines, in exchange for East and West Florida going to Britain.
- The Caribbean islands of Martinique, Guadeloupe, and St. Lucia were returned to France.
- France also kept Saint Pierre and Miquelon, a fishing outpost off Newfoundland.

French diplomat Étienne-François de Stainville, duc de Choiseul, chose to give up the vast Louisiana territory west of the Mississippi in exchange for France keeping the small Caribbean islands of Martinique, Guadeloupe, and St. Lucia. Canada had always been a drain on the French treasury, while Caribbean sugar was a booming business.

Spanish and French diplomats later on signed the Treaty of San Ildefonso, which treaty confirmed the ceding of French Louisiana to Spain.

Between Canada and the eastern United States, Great Britain gained control of enormous territory. Administrating the remote areas was an immediate problem for King George III.

In the coming years, disputes between the British Crown and the Thirteen Colonies arose over frontier policy, colonists' rights, and paying for the expenses of the Seven Years' War. These issues eventually led to a huge rift between both sides of the Atlantic.

After the Seven Years' War, the British prohibited speculative land companies from operating west of the Allegheny Mountains. Wealthy men in the Thirteen Colonies, including George Washington, were now prevented from obtaining title to the lands. Furthermore, the Crown ordered settlers who were living west of the mountains to pack up, abandon their holdings, and move back east—no matter how long they had been out west.

These and a host of other inconvenient policies began to mount in the minds of the colonists. Meanwhile, the Mother Country arrogantly assumed the colonists ought to be grateful to the Crown for its having freed North America of the French and ought to help pay for the war.

The two sides began to coalesce opposing perspectives. In Britain, the idea formed that the colonists were ungrateful and unruly. In the Colonies, the idea formed that the King and Parliament must be mad!

Significant events beginning in 1762 and continuing up through 1775 strained bilateral relations even further, until a conclusive breaking point came in 1776. These are the events that led to Revolution:

> 1764
> - The Sugar Act
> - The Currency Act
>
> 1765
> - The Stamp Act
> - The Quartering Act
> - Virginia Stamp Act Resolutions
>
> 1766
> - The Declaratory Act
>
> 1767
> - The Townsend Revenue Act
>
> 1770
> - Boston Massacre
>
> 1773
> - The Tea Act
> - Boston Tea Party
>
> 1774
> - The Intolerable Acts

- Declaration and Resolves of the First Continental Congress
- Battle of Point Pleasant (WV)
- Massachusetts colonists purchase arms and ammunition from Spanish merchant.

1775

- The Battle of Lexington and Concord
- Ethan Allen and the Green Mountain Boys seize Fort Ticonderoga.
- The Second Congress meets in Philadelphia & names George Washington as Commander-in-Chief.
- Patrick Henry speech – "Give Me Liberty or Give Me Death"
- Battle of Bunker Hill
- War of the Regulation
- Battle of Alamance

1776

- Publication of Thomas Paine's *Common Sense*
- The Virginia Declaration of Rights

- Declaration of Independence

The following pages describe the events in which Spain proved its value to America as Washington's Secret Ally during the Revolutionary War. It can be argued that without the assistance of Spain, U.S. independence would not have come to pass at that time. We quite possibly would still be flying the British flag!

Old World Background

When King Charles III[4], a Borbón, assumed the Spanish throne in 1758, he brought with him at least two principle desires: 1) to restore Spanish preeminence in Europe, and 2) to "stick it" to the British Empire, an adversary of old. In fact, Spain and England had repeatedly been at war with each other ever since 1337, the start of the Hundred Years' War.

In his own times, Charles III resented England for the outcome of the War of the Spanish Succession (1701-1713), which ended three years before his birth.

Even though the Treaty of Utrecht[5] brought the Spanish Borbóns to the throne, starting with Charles' father, Philip V, it

Charles III of Spain

simultaneously reduced Spain's power, glory, and influence across Europe.

Spain lost much of her European territories, including the Spanish Netherlands (Belgium) and parts of Italy. Other pieces she lost were Minorca and Gibraltar, both of which were given to her grand nemesis, Great Britain.

As Charles grew up, his resentment and passion grew up, too. He just couldn't stomach the thought that glorious Spain had been humiliated whilst his father sat on the throne. In 1734, as Duke of Parma, he conquered both the kingdoms of Naples and of Sicily and was crowned King of both on 3 July 1735. For the next nineteen years, he reigned as Charles VII of Naples and Charles V of Sicily.

From his residence in Naples, Charles kept tabs on his elder half-brother, Ferdinand VI[6], as the latter became King of Spain in 1746. Ferdinand VI has

Ferdinand VI of Spain

been described as a passive man. He ruled Spain for thirteen years. As King he worked very hard to keep Spain neutral in the years preceding the Seven Years' War. He refused tempting offers by both France and England into declaring war on the other.

Charles III was just the opposite.[7] After succeeding to the Spanish throne on 10 Aug 1759, he instigated a policy of "enlightened absolutism," which included several reforms and a build-up of the Spanish military. The forty-eight-year-old King was determined to take back Spanish pride. He expelled the Jesuits, and, in a move that wrecked his half-brother's tradition of neutrality, rekindled the Borbón Family Compact[8] with Louis XV of France.

The pact had been invoked twice in earlier times, and it was signed in secrecy a third time on 15 August 1761. It stipulated that all the Borbón kings (representing France and Navarre; Spain; the Two Sicilies; and the Duchy of Parma) would stand united, in defense of each other, and would put an end to British maritime supremacy. Thus, in 1762, Spain joined France against England and its ally Portugal in the ongoing Seven Years' War. By that time, France knew she was losing the war.

Louis VX of France

In September 1762, the French lost the Battle of Signal Hill (Newfoundland). At that point, Louis XV signaled to Charles III that he would cede to Spain the city of New Orleans and the whole of French territory west of the Mississippi in order to prevent their old nemesis from gaining full control of the strategic river.

Perhaps a concession of sorts from France to Spain, the land ownership was exchanged by the secretive Treaty of Fontainebleau of 1762; however, the change of title was not made public until 1764.

Meanwhile, the Treaty of Paris signed in February 1763 brought the Seven Years' War (French & Indian War) to an end and signified a major loss of territory for France. All of French North America east of the Mississippi was given to England, save for a couple of fishing outposts off Newfoundland and a few Caribbean islands.

Spain also lost territory east of the Mississippi. The treaty forced Spain to cede Florida to Britain, In exchange for its getting back the Philippines and Cuba, which the British had occupied. Losing Florida to the British was another loss of Spanish territory that King Charles III could not tolerate.

This 1779 engraving, published in London, shows the Devil joining France and Spain together

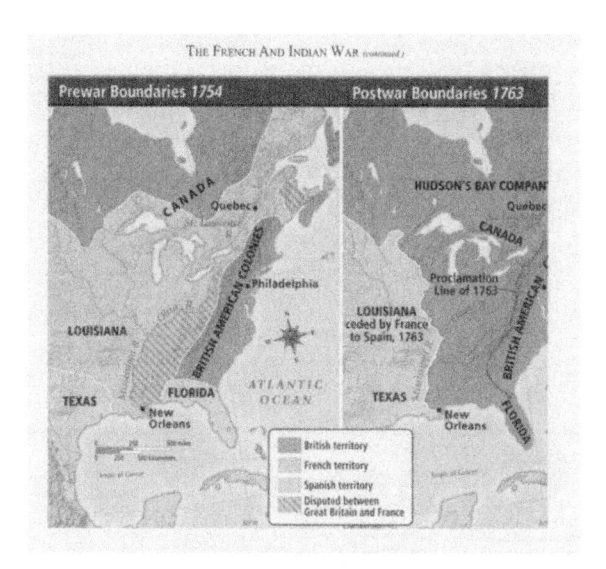

Maps showing land west of the Mississippi taken from France and given to Spain In 1763

Therefore, the two European powers that would come to the aid of the Thirteen Colonies were disgruntled old foes of the British Empire, just waiting for the day to regroup, revamp, and reconquer. The monarchs may have been empathetic to the Patriot cause, but they were first and foremost motivated by their relative positioning in the European balance of power. Both France and Spain, therefore, viewed the American Revolution within a global context of how best to weaken Britain all around the world.

Early Spanish Involvement

Even a year before the Americans declared their independence, the royal courts of France and Spain had committed to supporting the Patriot cause. The Continental Congress had sent diplomats to Europe as early as 1774, and one of the carrots which Benjamin Franklin and others dangled before the Borbón sovereigns was the promise to restore their North American territories to pre-Treaty of Paris designations.

At that hour, however, both monarchs intended to remain neutral in the looming war. International law banned neutral countries from providing money, arms, or ammunition to countries at war. So, any support they lent to the United Colonies in terms of money or materials had to be absolutely covert.

Benjamin Franklin

The Spanish monarchy was particularly concerned about maintaining secrecy. At that stage, Charles III certainly did not want to provoke a declaration of war on his kingdom by Britain's King George III. Britain's long-time standing ally was Spain's next-door neighbor, Portugal.

Given the situation, it was decided that financial and material support from Spain and France would have to be channeled through a third-party entity and appear as private business transactions. There were no restrictions on private citizens of neutral countries doing business with private citizens of belligerent nations.

A fictitious French merchant company called Rodrigue Hortalez & Cia.[9] in 1775 was established to make purchases, arrange for shipment, keep accounts, and contact American representatives in France. The playwright Pierre Augustin Caron de Beaumarchais was named as the firm's director. Both Borbón kings initially extended one million French Livres in seed money to Rodrigue Hortalez & Cia.

On top of that, Arthur Lee, diplomat from Virginia, secured an additional million Livres from Charles III. For the actual shipping of materials, both courts primarily used the Spanish firm of Joseph Gardoqui & Sons in Bilbao, Spain.

Diego Gardoqui, one of Joseph's sons, acted as representative to the Americans in Spain. He met with John Jay on several occasions and, after the Revolution, became Spain's first envoy to the United States.[10]

Historic letters prove that military supplies shipped by the Gardoqui firm had started flowing much before 4 July 1776. In a letter dated 15 February 1775, Diego Gardoqui responded to an order placed by Jeremiah Lee of Marblehead,

Massachusetts on behalf of the Massachusetts Committee of Supplies for over

Pierre Augustin Caron de Beaumarchais

Diego Gardoqui

three hundred muskets, three hundred bayonets, and six hundred pistols. In another example, on 29 July 1775, fourteen tons of gunpowder arrived in Philadelphia from Joseph Gardoqui & Sons and was immediately shipped to the rebels fighting in Boston.

In 1777 alone, Benjamin Franklin arranged for shipment through Gardoqui's firm of the following inventory:

- 215 bronze cannon

- 30,000 muskets
- 30,000 bayonets
- 51,314 musket balls
- 300,000 pounds of powder
- 12,868 grenades
- 30,000 uniforms
- 4,000 tents

Sometimes British ships would intercept arms and munitions meant for delivery to the fighting rebels. In the spring of 1776, an American merchant ship was detained near Boston transporting over twenty tons of gunpowder shipped from Gardoqui. Also captured in the spring of 1776 in Delaware Bay was a Spanish merchant ship with $14,000 in a box marked "W.M.," presumably belonging to William & Morris, another authorized shipper.

British diplomats in Spain and France knew of the movement of military stores across the Atlantic to the Thirteen Colonies and to Caribbean ports, but they could not prove the courts were financing it. Did they suspect it? Beyond his initial two million Livres for the merchant company, Charles gifted several more millions of Livres throughout the war to key individuals of the Patriot cause. In the three-year period 1776-1779, he loaned some eight million Spanish *Reales* to the Colonies.[11]

In addition to the money, munitions, and other materials, Spain gave immediate favored-nation trade status to the Americans, meaning all Spanish ports throughout her vast colonial empire were open to American shippers and traders. Not only were American ships welcome in Spain, but they also received open doors in places such as Havana, Cuba; Veracruz, Mexico, and New Orleans.

The Port of New Orleans was a key strategic location. In June 1776, September 1776, and June 1777 Spanish ships arrived into New Orleans laden with military supplies for the Continental Army. Those supplies were in turn shipped up the Mississippi and Ohio rivers to Fort Pitt. The American fiscal agent in New Orleans, Oliver Pollock, acted as intermediary between Spanish officials in Louisiana and the Continental Congress and Virginia. He worked indefatigably for the Patriot cause and fulfilled an extremely crucial, if not under-recognized, role in the chain of supply from New Orleans.

After the September 1776 shipment arrived there, Gen. Charles Henry Lee sent Capt. George Gibson with a small party down the Ohio and Mississippi to New Orleans to transport the supplies back upriver to Fort Pitt (Pittsburgh). Pollock introduced Gibson to the Spanish Governor of Louisiana, Luis de Unzaga y Amezaga, who politely agreed to look past the military goods being shipped upriver to Fort Pitt.

These early shipments to New Orleans included thousands of barrels of gunpowder. In fact, the rebel gunpowder used at Lexington-Concord and at Bunker Hill was most likely of Spanish origin.[12]

The Coat of Arms of Spanish Louisiana.
General Archive of the Indies, Seville

France Declares War On Britain

Spanish involvement in the Revolutionary War deepened after the Patriot win at the Battle of Saratoga (Oct. 1777), and it seems Spain even encouraged France to deepen its commitment prior to France's becoming a military ally.

In an October 1777 letter from Spanish Prime Minister José Moñino y Redondo, 1st Count of Floridablanca, to the French ambassador at Madrid, he states that a long duration of the American war would be "highly useful" to Spain and France. "We should sustain the Colonists, both with effectual aid in money and supplies" and with "prudent advice."[13]

Four months later, in February 1778, France signed treaties recognizing the United Colonies as an independent country and declared war on Britain. American and French diplomats on February 6, 1778, signed the Treaty of Alliance as well as the Treaty of Amity and Commerce. At the same time, it declared war against Great Britain.

Spain followed in 1779. But the Borbón Family Compact was not enough for King Charles III to risk going to war. By that time France had a new king, Louis XVI, who was Charles III's nephew. Charles was thirty-eight years older than Louis XVI, and at the time of his nephew's coronation, Charles had been a king for nearly forty years (he had been King Charles VII of Naples and Charles V of Sicily prior to assuming the Spanish throne).

Louis XVI pushed his uncle into signing the Treaty of Aranjuez, in return promising him that France would aid Spain in the capture and return of Gibraltar, Minorca, and Florida from the British.[14] This fed into Charles III's goal of redeeming his family's honor after Spain

Louis XVI of France

had lost both Minorca and Gibraltar on his father's watch and Florida on his own watch.

A European Front

After France signed the treaty, in April 1779, Spain then declared war on Britain and provided military assistance to the Patriots on several fronts. Together, Spain and France sought to tie up the British military in other parts of the world, so that their reinforcements to the Colonies would be harder to come by.

In August and September, 1779, the combined French and Spanish "Armada" alarmed the British people when it sailed into the English Channel and approximated the coastline in what was planned to be an invasion of Britain. Except for the flamboyant raids along the English coast of Captain John Paul Jones, this was the only potential invasion of

John Paul Jones

England that came out of the American Revolutionary War. Plagued by innumerable delays and poor weather, however, the invasion was eventually called off. Nonetheless, the show of strength caused sufficient enough concern on the home front that George III was forced to maintain a significant military presence in England.[15]

Immediately following the armada scare, John Paul Jones began his string of successful raids along the English coast. He also captured several British ships. His forays alarmed the military and helped turn the tide of public opinion on the war against the Crown. Jones was supplied by Gardoqui & Sons and used the Spanish port of La Coruna as a base of operations for eighteen months.

The most sustained effort by the allied navies to draw British firepower away from the Colonies, however, was the Great Siege of Gibraltar, 16 June 1779 - 7 Feb 1783. A battle of nearly four years in length, it occupied a large number of ships of the English navy and thereby kept those vessels (and men) away from the Colonies.

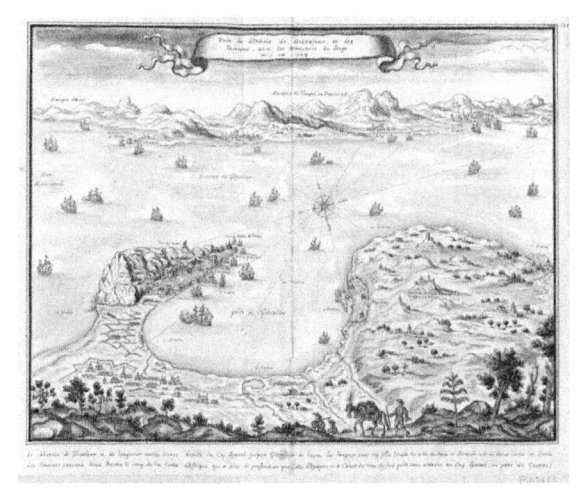

1704 engraving of Gibraltar, from a distance, by French artist Louis Boudan.

At one point, the combined Franco-Spanish army attacking Gibraltar totaled over thirty thousand men. Spain deployed fifty ships of the line and a large number of frigates. The effort was, to say the least, a large and ongoing strain for British forces.[16]

The Western Theater

Prior to and during the Revolutionary War itself, the lands along the Mississippi River were sparsely settled, with English outposts on the east bank and Spanish villages on the west bank. From south going north, the British controlled Manchac, Natchez, Memphis, Kaskaskia, Cahokia, Fort St. Joseph, and Detroit. Spain held New Orleans, Baton Rouge, Arkansas Post, St. Genevieve, and Fort San Carlos (Saint Louis, Missouri).

In 1777, the year after Spanish King Charles III named Bernardo de Gálvez y Madrid[17] as Governor of Louisiana, there were only 1,448 people registered as living in the Illinois country. Said region was the name attached to upper Louisiana. The King had sent Gálvez to Louisiana the prior year and had named him Colonel of the Louisiana regiment and second in command of provincial forces. Bernardo came from a distinguished and prominent family which had served the Spanish court in various ways. His father was the Governor of the Kingdom of Guatemala, which then encompassed all of Central America. His

Don Bernardo de Gálvez

uncle was Minister to Prussia, later Minister to Russia.

Before Gálvez left Spain, the king informed him directly that Spain would be entering into the hostilities between Britain and her Colonies, but to keep that a secret for the time being.

As the top commander in Louisiana, his duties were to develop and maintain friendly relations with the nearby Indians; to build good relationships with the nearby trappers and settlers, most of whom were French; to develop agriculture, and to recruit and train a militia. To help him and protect him, the King provided a small detachment of troops from the Royal Spanish army to accompany him.

After Bernardo arrived in Louisiana, two of the first things he did were to seek additional men to defend the frontier and to name a lieutenant governor for Spanish Louisiana. In response to his request for additional men, the Court promised him seven hundred volunteers from the Canary Islands for the Louisiana Infantry Regiment. These Canary Islanders were transported, starting in 1778, and many saw action in the Louisiana territory.

As for selecting the second-in-charge, Gálvez named Fernando de Leyba to the post.[18] Leyba was to superintend the affairs of the entire Louisiana territory extending from the Arkansas River to the Canadian line. In addition to being named Lieutenant Governor, Leyba was also appointed Commandant of Fort San Carlos, the Spanish fortress at the tiny village of St. Louis, and of St. Genevieve, an even smaller Spanish settlement about thirty miles south of Fort San Carlos. Although small, this fort played a huge role in the western theater.[19]

When de Leyba settled in at Fort San Carlos, he brought with him knowledge of the impending war between Spain and England. It wasn't long before he began to witness massive amounts of aid coming up river, bound for Fort Pitt at the Forks of the Ohio.

Early depiction of Saint Louis, with tower fortification in background, river in foreground. Image source: mssdar.org

Without revealing what he knew, Don Fernando began urging the townspeople to construct a series of four stone towers and entrenchments for self-defense. Many St. Louisans thought such preparations were foolish and a waste of money. They were convinced that their village would never be attacked, and that life would go on indefinitely the way it always had. Yet it was only a matter of time before storm clouds would gather and the earth would rumble:

the fortress and small village surrounding it were, in fact, sitting ducks, along a major, strategic transportation route which the British wanted to control.

Clark's Spanish Friends

Not long after Leyba arrived at St. Louis, he met George Rogers Clark, a lieutenant colonel of the Virginia militia who had been dispatched to the Northwest primarily to defend the newly created Kentucky County from hostile natives and to try to capture British villages north of the Ohio. Clark was a lot like Daniel Boone, in that he explored the backwoods far and wide and won the respect of nearly everyone he met.

In mid-1778, Clark had embarked with under two hundred men down the Ohio River, where they captured Fort Massac at the mouth of the Tennessee River before moving overland to take Kaskaskia (Illinois) on 4 July. Five days later, they took Cahokia. After that, he sent envoys to Vincennes on the Wabash River, and they brought back news of the town's allegiance to Virginia. Each of the three settlements had succumbed without a single gun being fired.

De Leyba was duly impressed with Clark's achievements, to say the least. During Clark's first visit to Fort San Carlos, Leyba ordered a two-day celebration, including an artillery salute, a formal dinner with thirty guests, and dances on two evenings followed by late suppers each night at Leyba's home. They became fast friends.

Over the years, de Leyba honored him with gala banquets, and the two men frequently corresponded. After Clark's death, his own family sustained that the general had long held romantic sentiments for de Leyba's sister.[20]

Through de Leyba and a former soldier of the Spanish army, Francis Vigo, Clark would receive much-needed supplies from Gálvez in New Orleans. Vigo had been a soldier in New Orleans but by then lived at St. Louis and had established a fur-trading business there. He, like Clark, knew the region well and knew the natives. Clark ended up recruiting Vigo to spy on the British, and Vigo also was wealthy enough to finance Clark's expedition.[21]

*The US Postal Office commemorated the memory of Francis Vigo with a stamp issued in 1986.
Image source: ebay.ie; accessed July 15, 2016*

In December 1778, Henry Hamilton, British lieutenant governor at Fort Detroit, departed with five hundred men down the Wabash River and easily retook Vincennes, which he renamed Fort Sackville.

Nevertheless, Hamilton was suspicious of him and told him not to "do anything injurious to the British interests on his way to St. Louis." True to his word, Vigo traveled to St. Louis before returning to Kaskaskia to inform Clark of the British hold on Fort Sackville.

Clark sent Vigo to scout out the fort and report back to him at Kaskaskia. But Indians captured Vigo once he arrived and turned him over to Hamilton. Since Vigo was a Spanish citizen and thus, in late 1778, a non-combatant, Hamilton was obliged to let him go.

Feeling uneasy, Clark marched his men for eighteen days through freezing and flooded terrain in February 1779 to retake the fort by surprise. Hamilton surrendered the next day. For those brave and trying exploits, Clark was hailed as a hero throughout Virginia. While Virginians were grateful to Clark, the Commonwealth had not supported his efforts with enough cash and supplies. Had it not been for Vigo, Leyba, and Gálvez, supplying him with materials, money, intelligence, and encouragement, it is highly doubtful that Clark would have been able to carry out his mission in the Illinois country.

Britain's Grand Design

By the end of 1779 and beginning of 1780, Britain had begun seriously eyeing the Mississippi Valley as a potential second front. From the Illinois country, they planned to sweep down the Mississippi to New Orleans, targeting Spanish settlements along the western side of the river and taking control of river commerce. By cutting off the strategic flow of weapons and supplies coming up the Mississippi, the British army would have been able to shut down a crucial supply chain and, effectively, surround the Continental Army. To carry out this strategy, they had to rely heavily on the assistance of their Indian allies.

It can be said one of Britain's greatest weaknesses (failures) in the American Revolution was their belief that Native Americans in the West and Loyalist sympathizers in the South would repeatedly risk their lives for the Crown's sake.

"Upon the declaration of war against Great Britain by Spain in 1779," writes the late historian Milo Milton Quaife, "Britain proceeded to plan a comprehensive campaign which would sweep the whole western American frontier from Canada to Florida and result in destroying the power of both Spain and the colonists in the Mississippi Valley.

"From Pensacola in the South and Detroit in the Northwest, as centers of operation, the British forces were to converge upon lower

Louisiana, having taken St. Louis en route," Quaife scribed.[22]

The British officer in charge of the campaign was named Emanuel Hesse. He set out in early 1778 with a few British regulars and over two hundred Indians from Northwest tribes hostile toward France.

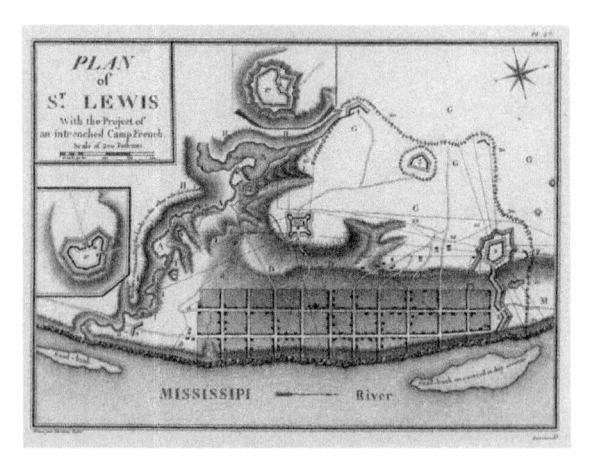

Map of St. Louis, 1790s. Library of Congress
Image source: loc.org

Meanwhile, Leyba appealed to the early St. Louisans to fund their village's own defense. In the end, though, he donated much of his personal money to the cause. Although he had wanted to build four stone towers, by mid-April of that year only one had been completed. It stood forty feet tall and measured thirty feet across. Leyba named it Fort San Carlos in honor of Charles III. The fort was located where Fourth and Walnut streets intersect today in downtown St. Louis.

In anticipation of Hesse's forces, de Leyba had three four-pound cannon and two six-pounders placed atop the fort. Tensions mounted in St. Louis, which was protected by only sixteen Spanish soldiers and the able-bodied men of the town's militia, mostly Frenchmen and Creoles. His intuition proved telling. On 26 May 1780, British-led Indians along with French-Canadian and British regulars indeed fell upon the vulnerable community in what is now called the Battle of San Carlos.

Hesse was so confident of victory that he even decided to divide his force. While the larger force was directed to St. Louis, a smaller force was sent to the American-held outpost at Cahokia. At Fort San Carlos, the attacking party reportedly numbered 1,300 - 3,000, consisting mostly of the British Indian allies. The defenders were greatly outnumbered. Nevertheless, they hit the attackers with a barrage of fire from their musketry as well as grapeshot from the tower's guns. Unaccustomed to facing the enemy from upon high, most of the attackers abandoned the field with haste. Leyba's defenses had won the day.

Mural of the Battle of San Carlos, Missouri State Capitol, Jefferson City. Image source: wikipedia.com

    Across the river, George Rogers Clark's men defended Cahokia and beat back the attacking party there as well. In upper Louisiana, then, the combined efforts of George Rogers Clark and his militia, Fernando de Leyba and his militia, and Francis Vigo, proved valiant enough to stop the Brits cold.[23]

    By this time, de Leyba's health had been deteriorating. His wife had already died in the Illinois country wilderness, and all he wanted was to take his two young daughters back to

Barcelona. That never happened. About a month after the long-anticipated battle, Fernando de Leyba was dead.

Gálvez' brilliant defense of lower Louisiana and along the Gulf Coast was yet to come.

Gen. Bernardo de Gálvez— Hero of the Battle of Pensacola

Horizontal rain pelted Gálvez during the night of 18 Oct 1780 and stung him like a thousand sharp needles. The rain was propelled by sustained winds of over one hundred seventy miles per hour. Saltwater burned his eyes. Rainwater and brine saturated his clothes. His hands were bloodied from holding so fast to the jack line.

The *San Juan Nepomuceno*[24] careened back and forth on a raging ocean, heaving up and down, slamming from starboard to port and back. At one point, the ship's wheel spun wildly out of the helmsman's control and broke his jaw. Water crashed onto the decks, sweeping away a junior officer and three twenty-four pounders.

The ship then plowed into another monstrous wall of water, which hoisted its stern out of the sea, nearly perpendicular. With the stern exposed, another wave came up and snapped off the ship's tiller. Now the *San Juan Nepomuceno*, its remaining crew, and its loosened cargo, were all at the complete mercy of the swirling elements…

†††

Rendering of the Spanish ship of the line,
San Juan Nepomuceno
Image source: seagifts.com

Gálvez had left Havana two days before, 16 Oct 1780, under calm conditions. The Governor of Spanish Louisiana and Field Marshal of the Spanish army in North America had disembarked with a fleet of sixty-two ships and four thousand fighting men. His objective: to launch a siege and invasion of Pensacola, the last stronghold for the British along the Gulf Coast.[25]

Although Spain had initially designated an impressive six regiments (seven thousand men) from the motherland to support this invasion, the sustained British siege on Gibraltar held them back for months. Finally the "Spanish Army of Operations" crossed the Atlantic, which took an additional three months. After enduring Gibraltar and the crossing of the sea, nearly the whole army fell deathly ill or succumbed to disease.

In the end, the great majority of Gálvez' four thousand soldiers had to be recruited from Puerto Rico, Cuba, Hispaniola, Venezuela, and México (New Spain).[26]

As the vessels headed north from Havana and crossed the wide Gulf Stream, an approaching hurricane engulfed the entire fleet,

Old Havana and Cathedral, Grisaille image by E. J. Meeker (c. 1922). Image source: ejmeeker.org/cuba

foiling Spain's first attempt to take Pensacola. Remnants of the damaged ships washed aground along the Gulf Coast, the Mississippi delta, the Florida Keys, and the Bay of Campeche, Mexico.[27] The outcome was a huge setback by any measure; nevertheless, it was not a defeat.

After the storm, Gálvez repaired what he could and sailed the *San Juan Nepomuceno* and remaining seaworthy ships back to Havana. He and his men spent a month regrouping the surviving fleet.

Five years prior to the Battle of Pensacola, in 1776, Col. Gálvez was sent to New Orleans for the first time. By the next year, at twenty-nine years old, he was appointed Governor of Spanish Louisiana.

He was named to the post when Governor Luis de Unzaga requested retirement. In an effort to cement stronger ties between the French citizenry and Spanish rulers, Unzaga had looked the other way whenever British ships approached New Orleans for trading purposes.[28] Gálvez, however, would not look the other way.

Indeed, Bernardo did much to aid the American patriots. He corresponded directly with Patrick Henry, Thomas Jefferson, and Charles Henry Lee, personally received their emissaries, Oliver Pollock and Capt. George Gibson, and responded to their pleas to block British watercraft from the Port of New Orleans. Gálvez often worked through brokers and carefully concealed the Spanish Court's involvement in covert operations.

Soon after taking over, he sent word to Madrid that a vast amount of Spanish soldiers were needed to defend the Louisiana territory, which was sparsely populated on the whole. He preferred soldier-colonists rather than mercenaries. The court responded by sending over seven hundred male volunteers and their families from the Canary Islands.

One of the five ships on which they sailed was the *San Juan Nepomuceno*. The total number of Canary Islanders in Louisiana reached twenty-three hundred persons. Many of them settled in St. Bernard Parish.[29]

The Texas Connection to the American Revolution

Following a devastating hurricane, in which all the cattle in Gálvez' herd were drowned and all the grain fields were flooded, he had to acquire beef and grain to feed his soldiers.

As a young cavalry officer in west Texas, Gálvez recalled the huge Texas Longhorn Cattle that were being grown in Texas.

In order to feed his troops, Gálvez sent an emissary, Francisco García, with a letter to Texas governor Domingo Cabello y Robles requesting the delivery of Texas cattle (Longhorns) to Spanish forces in Louisiana.[30]

Between 1779 and 1782, between 9,000 -15,000 head were rounded up and trailed to Nacogdoches, Texas, and to Natchitoches and Opelousas, Louisiana, for distribution to Gálvez' forces. Several hundred horses were also sent along for artillery and cavalry purposes. The Texans even provided enough hay and other grains to feed for the animals on their cattle drive, and to feed them until Louisiana could bring in another crop.[31]

First Church of Saint Louis, New Orleans. During six decades (1727-1788), French Governors Perier, Bienville, Vaudreuil and Kerlerec, and Spanish Governors Unzaga, Gálvez and Miro all worshipped at this church. Image source: stlouiscathedral.org

Spain Declares War

By 1778, after the theater of war shifted to the South and the Redcoats took Savannah and Charleston, the Patriots looked weak. They had lost thousands of men in the South and suffered through the replacement of two commanding generals.

The British began entertaining the idea of opening a western front. In October of that year, Lord George Germain ordered Brig. Gen. John Campbell, 17th Earl of Strachur, to take command of His Majesty's troops in West Florida. Germain instructed his Scottish general to "avoid disputes with, or giving occasions of Offense to, the Subjects of Spain."[32]

Gen. John Campbell, of Strachur

Nevertheless, by April 1779, the court in Madrid sent an ultimatum to the British. Among other stipulations, the Spanish demanded that the Thirteen Colonies be recognized as an independent nation. Unsurprisingly, the British rejected these terms and declared war. Spain responded with its own declaration of war, on 21 June 1779.

Less than one week later, Britain's King George III and Lord George Germain sent a top-secret letter to Campbell at Pensacola, instructing him that it was of greatest importance to organize an attack upon New Orleans. The top-secret communication was intercepted via Natchez and fell into Gálvez' hands.

Learning of this development, the "Spanish Savior" set out to stop the British cold. In September of that year, Gálvez marched more than a thousand men over a hundred miles northwest of New Orleans in eleven days. His troops included Spanish regiments and the remarkably diverse Louisiana Infantry Regiment, comprising Canary Islanders, Cajuns, French Creoles, English-Americans, Irish, Germans, Africans, and some Native Americans.[33]

They easily captured Manchac and took Baton Rouge by a ruse. In Baton Rouge, British Col. Alexander Dickson surrendered nearly four hundred of his regular troops; Gálvez had Dickson's militia disarmed, and he also negotiated for the transfer of Fort Panmure at Natchez, to Spanish control.[34]

The British flag would no longer fly anywhere in the Lower Mississippi region. Spanish flags were hoisted in their place.

Next Target: West Florida

With the river free, Gálvez set his sights on the Gulf Coast and West Florida. By 25 Feb, the Spanish had landed their army on the shores of the Dog River, about ten miles outside Fort Charlotte in Mobile.[35]

An enemy deserter informed them the garrison comprised an estimated three hundred men,

Capt. Elias Walker Durnford

compared to the twelve hundred men under Gálvez. Having such an advantage, the genteel Gálvez offered Capt. Elias Walker Durnford a chance to surrender, but Durnford graciously refused.

The outnumbered British resisted stubbornly until Spanish firepower breached the walls of the fort. At the hour of the siege, Durnford was still waiting in vain for relief from Pensacola, but the reinforcements that Campbell sent out were delayed *en route;* he was forced to surrender. On 14 March, Gálvez took the fortress.[36]

While in Mobile, the Spanish leader learned that additional British ships had arrived in Pensacola, including British Royal Navy vessels. Without naval reinforcements of his own, he left a garrison in Mobile and made a beeline for Havana to raise the troops and equipment needed for the coming showdown at Pensacola. Gálvez spent the winter in Cuba.[37]

The following spring, with the blessings of the regional *audencia*, he sailed a second time to Pensacola. He left Havana on 28 Feb 1781 with forty ships and over three thousand soldiers, including a Majorcan regiment, Spain's Irish Hibernia Regiment, and the Louisiana

1767 Map of West Florida
Source: University of Miami

militia. After some initial hesitation resulting from disputes between Gálvez and Captain José Calvo de Irazabal, the governor himself sailed his own vessel, the *Gálveztown*, through the straits.[38] The other ships followed his lead, and they landed at Santa Rosa Island to begin a two-month siege of three British fortresses, including Fort George.

By 23 April, reinforcements had arrived from Havana, increasing Gálvez' total force to *nearly eight thousand men*. On 8 May, a howitzer shell from the Spanish troops struck a British magazine, exploding it and killing fifty-seven.

The Spanish then opened fire with artillery on the next two British positions. The defenders were soon overwhelmed by the firepower, and, reluctantly, on 10 May, Gen. Campbell surrendered.[39]

*Spanish grenadiers and Latin American militia attacking the British at Pensacola.
U.S. Army Center for Military History*

None of these victories came easy. Gálvez and his men fought harsh conditions, faced multiple hurricanes along the way, and ran ships aground on sandbars at more than one approach. They often marched through brackish swamps, suffered shortages of supplies, and laboriously dug trenches or tunnels and created earthworks in preparation for repetitively sieging the enemy.[40] But at each location, Spain's army vastly outnumbered the enemy, and its artillery power was superior.

In Retrospect

The attack on Pensacola was the last offensive Gálvez oversaw in the Revolutionary War. It was the final victory in a string of victories that effectively dislodged the British from both the Mississippi and the Gulf Coast, squelching the enemy's fantastical plans to squeeze the Thirteen Colonies from the far western front. The outcome further accelerated the conclusion of the war between Britain and her Thirteen Colonies in America.

After the surrender, Gálvez and fleet returned to Havana and were welcomed as heroes. King Charles III promoted Gálvez to major general and made him governor of West Florida as well. With the conclusion of the Revolutionary War, he returned to Spain and received another hero's welcome, as well as an additional promotion to lieutenant general, appointment as captain general of Louisiana, Florida and Cuba, and elevation to the Viceroyalty of New Spain (Mexico).[41]

*Bust of Gálvez at Pensacola.
King Charles III granted the words, "Yo Solo," (By Myself)
be added to the Gálvez family's coat of arms.
Image source: rodurosa.blogia.com*

WANT TO KNOW MORE?

If this booklet has piqued your interest about General Bernardo de Gálvez and Spain's participation in the American Revolution, you will probably want to get the full story. Author and Judge Edward F. Butler, Sr. has written the complete story in *Gálvez / Spain - Our Forgotten Ally in the American Revolutionary War: A Concise Summary of Spain's Assistance*.

Thus far, his book has won five awards:

- *"Best American History Book about the American Revolutionary War in 2014"* awarded by The Texas Connection To The American Revolution
- *"Five-Star Award"* awarded by Readers' Review
- *"Presidio La Bahia Award"* awarded by The Sons of the Republic of Texas
- *"Best History Book in 2015"* awarded by the Texas Hill Country Chapter of Colonial Dames
- *"Best History Book in 2016"* awarded by Latino Literacy Now, organizer of the International Latino Book Awards

In addition to those five awards, the book has been given an Honorable Mention in the 2016 North Texas Book Festival's Book Awards for Adult Non Fiction.

Complete information about the book can be found at www.Gálvezbook.com. To order a copy, complete the form on the next page.

ORDER FORM

___ **Printed book ($29.00 each)** $_____

___ **Book on Searchable CD** $_____
    ($15 each)

___ **Printed Book & Book on** $_____
    Searchable CD ($39.00 set)

___ **Postage & Handling**
    ($6.50 each copy) $_____

TOTAL: $_____

Pay To The Order Of:
"Southwest Historic Press"

Mail Completed Form and Check to:

Southwest Historic Press
PO Box 170
24165 IH-10 West
Suite 217-170
San Antonio, TX 78257

End Notes

[1] The Gathering Storm is the title of Sir Winston Churchill's first book in his six book series on the history of World War II.

[2] The Winds of War is the title of an award winning book by Herman Wouk

[3] Of the two names for the same war, the former is the European reference, while the latter term is the preferred American reference.

[4] de Tapia Ozcariz, Enrique. *Carlos III y su época: Biografía del Siglo XVIII* (Aguilar, S. A. de Ediciones, Madrid) 1962

[5] Velde, François. "The Treaties of Utrecht (1713)", *Heraldica.org,* http://www.heraldica.org/topics/france/utrecht.htm

[6] Voltes Bou, Pedro. *La vida y la época de Fernando VI* (Editorial Planeta, Barcelona) 1998

[7] Wertz, W.F. "Spain's Carlos III and the American System—Spanish Participation in the American Revolution," Instit. Schiller, Washington, D.C., 2001

[8] Vaughan, Benjamin. *Remarks on a Dangerous Mistake Made as to the Eastern Boundary of Louisiana* (J.T. Buckingham, Boston) 1814

[9] Kite, Elizabeth S., *Beaumarchais and the War of American Independence* (Gorham Press, Boston) 1918; also, Rueda Soler, Natividad. *La Compañía de Comercio Gardoqui e Hijo: 1770-1780. Sus relaciones políticas y económicas con Norteamérica*
(Ediciones Gobierno Vasco, Vitoria) 1992.

[10] Gartiez-Aurrecoa, Divar Javier. "El embajador Don Diego María de Gardoqui y la Independencia de los EE.UU.," University of Deusto, Bilbao, Spain, 2003

[11] Fernandez y Fernandez, Enrique. *Spain's Contribution to the Independence of the United States* (Embassy of Spain, Washington, D.C.) 2000

[12] *Handbook of Texas Online,* Robert H. Thonhoff, "Galvez, Bernardo de," accessed Feb 07, 2016; also, Robert H. Thornhoff, "Vital Contribución de España en el Triunfo de la Revolución Americana," Karnes, Texas, 2006

[13] Allen W. Gardner, *A Naval History of the American Revolution*, Vol. 1 (Houghton Mifflin & Co., 1915), p. 334.

[14] Charles Edward, *Leading American Treaties* (Macmillan, 1922), pp. 24-25.

[15] Edward G. Gray, Jane Kamensky, *The Oxford Handbook of the American Revolution* (OUP USA, 2013), p. 322.

[16] Richard Van Alstyne, *Empire and Independence: The International History of the American Revolution* (New York: Wiley, 1965), pp 248-249.

[17] John Walton Caughey, *Bernardo de Gálvez in Louisiana, 1776–1783* (Berkeley: University of California Press, 1934); also, Lorenzo G. LaFarelle, *Bernardo de Gálvez: Hero of the American Revolution* (Eakin Press, 1992).

[18] Coughey, pp. 82, 95, 165-166.

[19] Robert B. Roberts, *Encyclopedia of Historic Forts*: "The Military, Pioneer, and Trading Posts of the United States," (Macmillan, 1988), pp 255, 325.

[20] James Alexander Thorn, *Long Knife, The Story of a Great American Hero, George Rogers Clark* (Ballantine Books, 1986), pp. 198, 230, 411.

[21] Dorothy Riker, "Francis Vigo," Indiana Magazine of History, Volume 26, Issue 1 (Indiana University, 1930), pp 12-24.

[22] Milo Milton Quaife, *Chicago and the Old Northwest, 1673-1835: A Study of the Evolution of the Northwest Frontier* (University of Chicago Press, 1913), p. 94.

[23] Thomas E. Chavez, *Spain and the Independence of the United States: An Intrinsic Gift* (University of New Mexico Press, 2004); *Missouri, A Guide to the Show-Me State*, American Guide Series (Oxford University Press, New York, 1941).

[24] Lorenzo G. LaFarelle, *Bernardo de Gálvez: Hero of the American Revolution* (Austin: Eakin Press, 1992)

[25] Hubert L. Koker, "Spanish Governor Bernardo de Gálvez Salvaged the Gulf Coast for the Future United States," *Military History* (June 1993)

[26] Chavez; LaFarelle; also, Barbara A. Mitchell, "America's Spanish Savior: Bernardo de Gálvez," *The Quarterly Journal of Military History* (Autumn 2010)

[27] Ibid.

[28] Ibid.

[29] Chavez; Granville W. Hough and N.C. Hough, *Spain's Texas Patriots in its 1779-1783 War with England - During the American Revolution, Sixth Study of the Spanish Borderlands* (Society of Hispanic Historical and Ancestral Research, 2000); also, Thornhoff.
Thornhoff

[30] Chavez; Hough; Thornhoff

[31] Ibid.

[32] George C. Osborn. "Major-General John Campbell in British West Florida." *Florida Historical Quarterly* (April 1949)

[33] Chavez; Hough, Thornhoff

[34] Osborn

[35] Chavez; LaFarelle; Mitchell

[36] Ibid.

[37] Ibid.

[38] Ibid.

[39] Ibid.

[40] Ibid.

[41] Ibid.